Poems fr[...]

by John Medl

I want to dedicate this book to my parents, family, and friends who have never left my side through my battles with mental illness. I also want to dedicate this book to the millions of people who suffer from mental illness around the world. I hope I have done well in being the voice of the suffering.

This is the second book I have written. My first book is titled, "Millions Like Me: My Struggle with Mental Illness". That's my whole life story up until 2013. This book is a book of poetry, with commentary mixed in. For clarity purposes, I wanted to give you a brief introduction. I have been writing poems since grade school. I am now 35 years old. These are all the poems I could find. There is no real order to any of the poems. I hope that my commentary will help clarify what I was thinking and feeling at the time. In 2006, I was diagnosed with bipolar disorder with psychotic features. Since 2006, the doctors have added Post Traumatic Stress Disorder, Generalized Anxiety Disorder/Panic Disorder, Obsessive Compulsive Disorder, agoraphobia, and claustrophobia. For the full story, reference my first book. I wanted a book completely devoted to the poetic arts. Just as with my first book, I hope this book leaves a positive, lasting impression on the readers.

Navigating Troubled Waters

A boat I have elected myself the captain

Attempting to steer ashore

The turmoil rising from below

The thunder pounding from above

I am surrounded---

And I am supposed to find land?

The sea sees no penalty when chaotic

But woe to the mind when disturbed

Shaken off course---

With an earthquake off the charts

My whole functioning without the parts

Vital to survive and succeed.

A persistent bleed from my heart through my skin

So the heart is where I shall begin

To repair what has failed for years.

I have survived typhoons and tidal waves countless times

I have crossed uncrossable lines

And disaster has gratefully let me prepare

For the misfortunes fortunate enough to plague me.

An easy task for they have seen stronger

But they will not weaken me a minute longer

Unknown, a formidable enemy clenches his fist

Executing his plans down the list.

The resilient may at first seem meek

The strong at first, weak

But victory hides in the end

A winner wins at the finish of a race

Not the beginning, soon to be erased.

Others are happy just to place

But winners all the same.

A spirit deserving of a name

But no one word could do justice

Call it a spark or flame

They wonder whom to blame

For these countless, relentless tries--

The sun dies, the wind cries, and the sea subsides.

You will not hold me back, turbulent sea

For my soul will set fire

As the kindling lay before me.

Fuel for my motor

A motivation unseen by woe or worry

A whirlwind of fury---

Let it strike down

Those who dare subjugate me

Under an umbrella of expectations

That even God would fall short.

But I will not, I refuse

To let abuse abuse me

I remain untouched and will forever be.

This was the first poem I ever had published in 2004, two years before I was diagnosed with bipolar disorder. I remember that this was an assignment for one of my poetry classes at the University of Dayton. This is one of my most polished poems, for it was edited several times before publication. I remember that when I wrote this poem, I felt like there was so much chaos in my life--- attending college full-time, and working full-time. I also had a live-in girlfriend, and I was constantly drinking alcohol and smoking marijuana. I was barely sleeping. I did this for almost three years straight. I believe that this chaos was a catalyst in making me ill, but no one really knows.

July 31, 2006

It was like lightning

Struck my brain in two

A feeling I hope never happens to you.

Fueled by a combination

Of drugs and chemical failure

I never even saw it coming.

But in hindsight, they say things seem clearer

The teamwork of genetics, environment, and behavior.

A complete mental meltdown

Of someone competent and capable before

Never having a clue of what tests were in store.

I thought I would get better soon

Not months, into years and more.

Confused, never in control

As the toxic cocktail took its toll

Crammed in a cell and then a bus to court

With total strangers, not knowing what I'd done

Or where I was

But knowing it wasn't normal or fun.

They had me sign some papers

That I couldn't focus to read

And plunged a needle deep in me

And gave me pills they said I'd need.

They took me to a ward where I was greeted

By shrieking vocal cords

They gave me a room, and a short tour

Life as I knew it, never more.

A condition I guess they thought they could fix

July thirty-first, two-thousand and six.

This is the day that I was rushed to the hospital, and then diagnosed with bipolar disorder with psychotic features. I had to stay in the psychiatric unit for eleven days. I would have to be hospitalized a few times after this too. I haven't been hospitalized since 2012. On that occasion, it was for mania and anxiety/panic. The doctors called it my "first break", which basically means the symptoms of bipolar disorder had become so severe that I was a danger to myself and others and needed to be hospitalized.

Quilted Sofa

Padded checkers and rings

Hold my see-saw feelings

Tragedy, triumph, good, and bad

The best rest I've ever had.

Once glued, now improved

I got back everything

I used to groggily wish for.

Now I seem to be

Trapped in my own clarity.

Truths that will haunt me for years, and fears, dried

up tears

Steered by sanity now, but how?

No better time to start than now

Forcing me to stand pat

A curse worse than a black cat

Labels by faces, replaces

All the old thoughts about myself.

But I know who and what I am

Like it or not

Do you really think my soul forgot?

After I was released from the hospital in 2006, I was heavily sedated. I slept on the sofa mentioned in this poem most of the day. All I could manage was to eat and go to the bathroom for the most part.

Medicinal Haze

I wake up in a medicinal haze

Left over from the night

And remember all the happy days

And all the ways I used to cope.

Those were times filled with hope.

Now instead of being free,

The doctors pump me full of dope.

With the stroke of his pen

He can control my behavior

Like some holier-than-thou savior.

Saving me from myself

Maybe I did need help

Maybe I'll be better off.

Some people hear disorder

And think it can be cured

Like a cold or cough.

But it will never go away, never will

At least the drugs keep me still.

Too still sometimes, more like a zombie

I guess the challenge is

Finding a balance between the new and the old me.

I remember writing this poem on a regular old morning. I was still pretty heavily sedated. I was learning to adjust to my "new self", i.e. how the drugs had changed me.

Just A Park

The sycamore and oak trees

Bow and wave to greet me

And immediately their presence

Makes me feel at peace.

One of my sanctuaries

I've been visiting for years

Not one tall building or store around

Just the trees and me

The rustling of leaves, the only sound.

Just a quiet spot to simply think

That's all I was really after

No music, conversation, or laughter.

No one to judge me by my fame or wealth

Or to criticize and scrutinize my health

Fields and woody statues

As far as I can see

At this place, in this time,

I can't think of a place I'd rather be.

When I started to become a little more alert, I used to drive to this park about ten minutes from my house. I would just read a book or write poetry or just sit peacefully and be one with nature. I remember feeling very at peace there. It was near a place called Camp Dennison, near a town called Indian Hill. I haven't been back in years. I need to find time to visit again.

Poser Friends

Self-reflection has revealed

An ejection of delusions and false hope.

A more quiet way to cope

Than screaming what I really think of you.

You are the weaker link of a chain now broken

Not even a sentimental token am I left with

A revelation freed from a dark hole

Like a mole, poking its head out for air

Far away in some hand-me-down chair

If you only knew what you lost

But that's just my perception

No better than the rest, no exception

You are no better friend than I am to you

Never have been

I'd like to cram, all your lies back in your mouth

One by one, 'til you choke

Our "friendship" was just a horrible, cruel joke.

Thanks, once again, poser friend

Your memory will never make me laugh again

I must have run out of what you wanted

Or you would still be around.

All I can say, and I hope you take with you

As penance for all your faults

Locked down tight in mental vaults

I could delicately unravel

But I would rather see you crack and explode.

Blow the doors off, and the landing won't be soft, no loft

Smack against a wall

I could watch you fall over and over again

I saw the end from afar

And now I'm glad to see who you really are.

You piece of nothing, trash on the street

Rancid and sour

And in your final hours, you can explore

The dark abysses you created

And I'm elated to see you doing so poorly.

I used to be concerned surely

When you were someone else…

I was angry at some of my "poser friends" that had left my side when I really needed them. The type of people who claimed to be my friends, but then left my side when I was sick.

There Is Hope

I lose my mind from time to time

But I always seem to find it

I sometimes get excited about the future

But my past looms right behind it.

Pain that pity and recovery can't resolve

An assortment of memories involved

And plans that never blossomed.

But if anyone thinks for one second

I will give up my hopes and dreams

Just to spite the daily screams.

There's just some things I can't repress

I try to give my all and nothing less.

When I started to come out of "the fog" of the sedatives, I was feeling hopeful because my life was starting to come back together again. I want everyone to know that there is life beyond mental illness, and that "there is hope".

Standing Tall

My head is pounding

And my mind won't quit

The hospital and medications

All because of it.

The sirens scream

Getting closer and closer

Until they are clear as can be.

You can imagine my terror

When I knew they were coming for me.

Laid out on a stretcher

Gasping for air

I wanted to be anywhere but there.

Every second felt like ages

And not a thousand pages

Could capture

How it has come to this.

Never a day goes by

When I don't obsess about it all

But through every single battle

At least I've stood tall.

I've had thousands of panic attacks. This is how I felt during and after. I remember hearing the sirens of the ambulance. I remember not being able to think clearly. At the end of this poem, I'm trying to make myself feel better by thinking and feeling, "At least I've stood tall", and that I have put up a fight.

Came from a Long Way

When I feel down,

I go back to that place.

The needles and doctors

My mind can't erase.

My concerned friends and family

Who came to visit,

And how my entire life

Is wrapped up in it.

It's everything to me.

It's what drives me to be

A good person and friend.

A success story.

I was down on the mat,

But I got up.

I don't know how or why.

I could have easily given up

And kissed my future goodbye.

I must not be done yet

Or else it would have ended.

My dreams aren't gone,

They just got suspended.

I gave it everything I had

I reached down deep

The memories still haunt me

Even in sleep.

When I have a bad day,

It can always be worse

The curse of making it through.

I give it all I've got

In everything I do.

This is describing my Post Traumatic Stress Disorder that I have from being in the hospital several times, with a touch of hope at the end. My PTSD results in flashbacks and nightmares. I have severe anxiety when I am confronted with anything medically related, or anything that resembles the experiences I've had in hospitals.

Monster of Pain

Behind the laughter and the smiles

There is pain for miles

I've cried so many times

Pleading it will stop.

It always seems to

When it wants to.

Most people don't know what makes me tick.

I don't even know if I do.

Maybe some day I will find out

How and why I got sick.

Maybe because I used to take life for granted

I never appreciated the little things

I just went about going through the motions

Never noticing anything surrounding the path I was on.

Most people have never seen me cry

I hide my emotions well

Every day is as big as a mountain

But you will probably not be able to tell.

My life's an open book

For everyone to read

I like it that way

Nothing to hide

Everything to explain

Like why sometimes

I prefer the rain.

Or why I value the company of friends so much

Or how my thoughts got out of touch.

Around 2011-2012, I started advocating for mental illness and telling my story. This poem touches on that a bit. When I finally started to "snap out of it", I decided I wanted to be an advocate. I still am to this day, in 2017. I talk about basically putting on a tough front so others don't seem to notice that I am struggling. I wonder what makes me tick, and I wonder if my mental illness is somehow a punishment because I took life for granted when I was younger.

Brain on Fire

My brain is on fire and my mind won't quit

Sometimes, I get sick of all of it.

I fight and I fight, but sometimes it's not enough

I just want to be known as tough.

I have a sense of humor to keep it light

I just want to do what's right.

My purpose is to make people smile and laugh

In that, I firmly believe

You can have all the money and all that comes with it.

I just want to leave a legacy of great stories.

That's what I want to achieve.

That others will commit

To their memories and have a lasting impression in their hearts.

At one time, I was torn apart.

I keep getting up and sometimes I don't know why or how

But I'm a lot closer to knowing now.

This poem is about how I want to be remembered. One of my life goals is never to be forgotten, or at least not for a very long time. I want to be known as tough and as someone that didn't give up. I want to be that person that makes the best of a bad situation. I talk about finding myself in this battle at the end of the poem. I allude to this battle as being something that has happened for a reason.

Small Town Man

Right near where the local roads meet the highway,

A man sits and thinks.

He is well-known around his home,

But the small town could not keep him forever.

One day, his name will be heard for miles

And all he can do is smile

Because he knew it would happen all along.

He had dreams about being famous

As long as he could remember

And everything was falling into place.

Not much grace, but there was something special about him.

Intangible, but real.

He could steal hearts in a matter of moments

And he would keep them forever

Because he was loving and loyal.

Far from royal, but he had a distinct strut

Like he had just won at a game.

Many people seem the same, so he sought out the

different to be his friends.

He couldn't care less about trends.

Or money, houses, or cars.

He liked to look up at the stars.

He survived on a little, but it felt like a lot to him.

He knew what it was like to have nothing,

And that feeling always stayed with him.

It helped him be humble and grateful.

Loving, not hateful. Positive, not skeptical.

He never wanted to be a spotlight spectacle.

Just always in others' thoughts

And hopefully those thoughts are fond.

And every time it was needed,

He would answer the bell and respond.

I have a nice front porch on my house that I like to sit and think and smoke cigarettes. This poem describes my desire to be somewhat famous, but not valuing material things. I want to be well-known, but remain humble. You will definitely keep seeing the theme of me not wanting to be forgotten any time soon, and to be remembered in a positive light, which really relates to my obsession with death and dying.

Beach

The sun shoots its rays

Across the expansive sky

Reflected off the water like glass

And I start to wonder why.

Anyone would wake to anything else

The clouds hanging over like cream

This is the morning most are forced to dream.

For some, an actuality

But they probably stopped looking

Thinking about bills, or errands for the day

While the sorrowful are longing

For such a sight to behold.

A scene, to some, has turned old.

But if I ever have a chance

To hear the waves crash and see the foam dance

The amazing sun and clouds overhead

I will rush to meet the sea.

But then what would I think about

To keep me restful in my bed?

I live in Cincinnati, Ohio, so I am far from the ocean. This poem is basically just me describing a daydream about the beach and ocean. I describe the daydream, but then wonder if it would be ruined if I actually got to experience my daydream (i.e. "but then what would I think about to keep me restful in my bed?").

Let Me Go

If you are done with me, let me go.

I've died several times.

I obsess over death. I dream about it.

I pray for it.

Until that time comes, let me live.

I don't want to be here halfway.

I have a job to do, and we both know it.

I need all the strength and courage I can hold.

I will leave nothing left untold.

My soul was meant to be shared.

It was really never mine.

It wasn't supposed to be like this, but here we are.

I've already come so far.

Don't let me go just yet. I have work to do.

I just need a little relief.

Forgive me for my beliefs, and all I have done wrong.

I want my list of good deeds to be long.

So when we meet, I can stand proud.

So when I sing, I can sing out loud.

The only thing I have ever been sure of is that I

wanted to be a good person

And help those in need.

Why must I bleed?

This poem is about my frustration with struggling to do small tasks. I am frustrated, but at the same time, I have "work to do" (advocate for the mentally ill). I am almost pleading to God, or gods, or the Fates, to "let me go, if you are finished with me". This also fits the theme of death that you have seen in other poems.

Broken Down

I feel broken

Usually unspoken.

It's a trembling,

Sometimes it seems unending.

My chest hurts,

In short bursts,

But I've learned it's not alarming.

It's disarming, I'm charming,

When I feel like myself.

And it all figures somehow

But don't ask me how.

I'm dizzy, light-headed

Scary memories, embedded.

I can't shake it, or take it

I just try to survive and make it.

I feel shattered,

I matter,

At least that's what they tell me.

I don't trust my instincts,

Or gut feels

My mind runs like hamster wheels.

It's be nice not to think at all for a while

And when I hit a wall,

I go around it or through it.

It's like I always knew it.

This is basically just how I feel on a regular basis. This alludes to racing thoughts ("my mind races like hamster wheels"), and also mania, where it's hard to trust my own judgment (instincts).

Lucky Stars

As I've gotten older

I carry around the hurt

As a chip on my shoulder.

I carry it around as a fire inside

When it starts burning

There's nowhere to hide.

I carry it around

As a weight on my back

Sometimes I can't shake it

Sometimes I look back.

I carry it around

Like concrete in my shoes

Hard to move forward

But refusing to lose.

Making giant steps

Stumble by stumble

Sometimes it's too much

But it keeps me humble.

A mind that doesn't stop

Cranking and cranking

It keeps me occupied

And it keeps me thanking

My lucky stars

For what could have been.

How it could be.

I focus more on that

Than how it should be.

This poem is about having a positive attitude, and never giving up. I allude to focusing on how it is and how it should be. I don't think it's therapeutic to think of the way things should or could be. I don't think it's productive to think life's not fair. I think it's in my best interest to deal with life as it has been given to me.

Child Giant

They all knew

He didn't belong

In a chair, anywhere

The desk wouldn't even hold him.

He sat in discomfort

Most of the time

And the teachers would often scold him.

He towered over the children

And more wit than the teachers

He disobeyed most rules

And challenged the preachers.

He was told things he had already been taught

Five years earlier, and never forgot.

A class clown

And a teacher's pet

All the lessons he would never forget.

A kind and gentle giant of a child

Calm and collected, with a touch of wild

Slow to anger

Quick to peace

A hunger for knowledge

Never ceased

This is my perception of how I was when I was a child. Or maybe other people's perception. In a way, it is arrogant to think I didn't belong "in a chair, anywhere" (i.e. a desk as in school). People with bipolar disorder often think highly of themselves. Also called grandiose feelings.

My Darkest Hour

And in my darkest hour

You had a kind word

My brain wasn't working

But I somehow still heard.

I remember your smiles

When my memory was lost

I remember the visits

At such a cost.

I remember your concern

At every single step

I remember how sad you were

Even while I slept.

I'll never forget

When you gave me your heart

Even when our souls

Were miles apart.

Even then

I still never forgot

All the love you gave

Towards the story, and the plot

I'm here today

Doing pretty well

Mostly because of you

And partly from going through hell.

There will still be those that don't believe

Everything I say

I've had some awful moments

And I still count the days.

I've learned a great deal

About life and about myself

I've taken all your acts

And placed them on a shelf

Any given moment

I can reach back in time

And remember what you gave me

Truly sublime.

This poem is about all the support I have received since 2006 from family and friends. It's worth mentioning that some people with mental illness have little to no support.

Wondering about Everything

Many times a day I wonder

How many nights I have left

I wonder if I would even want to know.

I wonder if I am living right

When the world tells me 'no'.

I wonder if Fate will smile kindly on me

And let me be around.

I wonder if I have done enough work

Before they lay me in the ground.

Or let the wind take my ashes to the sea

That's really the only place I wish to be.

I try to imagine how far the stars are away

And if I will get to see one up-close some day.

I only know how to live one way---

The simplest way I possibly can.

And at the same time

Leaving the Earth a good man.

Here is the theme of not being forgotten easily again. I often think about death. It's listed as one of the symptoms of bipolar disorder. Death or dying is a theme that you will see.

Death Stare

Only when you've stared death in the face

And survive

Only then are you truly alive.

Live like it is your last day

Don't make it something you just say.

I know this from experience

It's not some theoretical idea to me

I consider it a blessing to be

Reminded so soon of my mortality.

Some sail through life, no worries, and that's great

But this is not a lesson you want to learn late.

Let me be an example

And lend your ear

The struggles I have had, I hope you are never near.

And to you, I say good luck

Painting the canvas of life

And I hope your days are filled

With not a bit of strife.

But if life deals you an altering hitch

I can only wish

You find the strength to carry on

May all your troubles be short, and your days be long.

This is me trying to be positive after a panic attack. I truly wish the best for everyone. That is another theme you might see. I have a lot of love in my heart, despite everything.

While in Sleep

Words that are jumbled

Explosions of neon greens...

And brilliant bursts of blue.

A nervous, unsettling, spasm of moves.

Sleep comes in spurts

But it's never enough.

Dreams hardly come

And nightmares are plenty.

Wide awake and sweating.

The damage has been done.

If only memories had filters

And we could pick and choose

The ones to forget, and the ones we don't want to lose.

Work with what you're given,

As hard as that may be

You may find it will suffice.

Always know your worth

But never tag yourself a price.

I wrote this poem after a bad night's sleep. I try to be encouraging as well. There is another theme. Sometimes when I close my eyes, I see colors that I can only describe as pink and blue cotton candy, and they burst and dance like some kind of visual effects show.

The Graveyard Dancers

If life's so easy

And not so hard

Why do I believe

They are dancing in the graveyard?

Laughing when we drive past

With convincing looks it will all last

Stress and anx blur our thoughts

At least the dead are never lost

And never feel the need for greed

No violence or destruction

Not to ever have to bleed

Or the pressure to succeed.

If you deem these thoughts bizarre

Try looking out from the graveyard.

Here is the theme of death and dying again. I wrote about wondering if the dead have any pain or problems. I also wonder if I would be better off dead because at least I wouldn't be suffering.

The Winds of Love

His heart settled for a draw,

But it felt more like a loss.

He tried to adjust his sails,

But the winds of love

Would just blow across.

He could only do things halfway

Because he never felt complete.

He found solace in solitude,

And the material world could not compete.

He surrounded himself in knowledge,

And learned and taught many things.

But he could never find, in any book,

The joy that love brings.

This is about the heartbreak of not being able to find love in a mate. I also don't value material things too much anymore. I love learning, and I'm still unsure whether solitude is what I want.

Man on a Mission

I hope Heaven and Hell can wait.

I hope I arrive surrounded by love and late.

It's not my decision,

I'm just a man on a mission.

My life is in the hands of Fate.

I hope Heaven and Hell can wait.

This is another poem about my mortality. I feel like my "mission" is to be a mental health advocate and spread the word about mental illness.

Soar into the Heavens

I hope I soar into the heavens

Far above the sky.

I know I'll see all the angels

That too early, passed us by.

I want to meet all the saints

And ask them a lot of questions

Maybe over a nice dinner

And talk about the people I want to mention.

Maybe it will be an ocean

And I'll fall into the darkest depths

A peaceful place of silence

Filled with tears we all wept.

But maybe I'll be sent to Hell

The fire and smoky air---

A place for only a few

But I think I've already been there.

Here is the theme of death again and me wondering about the afterlife. Also describing the "Hell" that I have been through.

A Sturdy House

I built a house made of paper,

But it all came crashing down.

It all came crashing down.

I drove a car as far as I could drive,

But I wrecked along the way.

I wrecked along the way.

I took a bus to the end of the line,

But it went spinning of the road.

Spinning off the road.

I took a plane to the edge of the world,

But it fell before I got there.

It fell before I got there.

I built a boat that could stand a mighty wind,

But it sank to the bottom.

It sank to the bottom.

I built a life made of promises and hope,

But it all came crashing down.

It all came crashing down.

And then I stopped building,

And I just started creating things.

And nothing could bring them down.

Nothing could bring them down.

This is a celebration of the creative arts, and the denouncement of material things.

If It's the Last Thing I Do

If it's the last thing I do,

Let it be kind,

So I can have a clear mind.

If it's the last thing I do,

Let it be courageous

Because no one respects a coward.

If it's the last thing I do,

Let it be out of love

Because I want to leave it all for you,

And I have so much to give.

If it's the last thing I do,

Let it be noble

Because I want to leave proud.

If it's the last thing I do,

Let it show my strength

Because I have the heart of a lion.

If it's the last thing I do,

Let it be thoughtful

Because my intentions are good.

If it's the last thing I do,

Let it be creative

Because I have so much to share.

If it's the last I do,

Let it show character.

And if it's the last thing I do,

Let it be memorable.

Common themes of death and being remembered are repeated again here. Also my unwillingness to quit.

The Terror of Panic

In that place

All I feel is fear

And thoughts about death

Are near.

When it is through,

I just want to cry.

Another step backwards

Telling myself all I can do is try.

Enough to bring a big man

To his knees

And pray for it to be over

Begging for the end, please!

A terror so potent

Minutes feel like days

Feelings so strong

My ego always pays.

I never know when it will come

I just know I'm grateful when it's done

I sometimes wish I were the only one.

I just want someone to tell me it's okay

I just want the words to help convey

How awful the panic really can be

If you could only see

How crippling it really is

How painful and strong.

Not matter how short, it always seems long.

And I always feel wronged.

What did I do?

I try to be a good person

And do what's right

I try and work hard

And I'm thankful at night.

I know deep down it's not my fault

But I always retrace my actions

And my past deeds

Even though I know

I can't go back

I think if I do enough good

I can cover my tracks.

But the fact is,

Nothing I did

Has anything to do with me now

For some reason, I have been chosen

To make lemonade somehow.

I don't want your pity

That's not the point

I can't say enough

To get anyone to feel how terrible it can be

I wouldn't wish it on my worst enemy.

My description and feelings about a panic attack.

Life Creeps Up

We all want perfect little lives,

With everything in a row,

But that's rarely how it goes.

Life creeps up, and life creeps in,

And it forces us to change plans.

Some things are best unplanned,

While others seem too much to bear.

We are left gasping for air,

But soon it all passes.

And we start to pick up the pieces,

Pretending nothing ever happened.

But then, life creeps up, and life creeps in,

Forcing us to change the plans again.

This poem is about how life can be very unorganized, as much as we want everything planned out.

Not a Time for Sympathy

I don't need your sympathy.

I'll make some coffee

And have a cup with me.

Our roads crossed for some reason

Time don't matter or the season

But I don't need your sympathy.

We can talk until our tongues go dry

And if we need to

We can wipe each other's eyes.

I just love your company

But I don't need your sympathy.

I'll light a smoke while you're talking

And I'll listen the best I can

I want to hear your point of view

And all the things that make up you

But I don't need your sympathy.

I don't have close to all the answers

But maybe we have some common ground.

I just want to make you feel better

I know pain and I know healing

But I don't need your sympathy.

Our talk is over now and it's time to go

Maybe we can do this again

If I say I am your friend,

I will be one to the end,

But I don't need your sympathy.

This poem is about how I don't want people to feel sorry for me, and how I am almost always available to listen to a friend's problems. Also, that I enjoy just sitting and talking about life and whatever else. On a lighter note, I really enjoy coffee and smoking cigarettes on my front porch.

Psych Ward

Nightmares from the psych ward....

Nightmares from the psych ward....

Flashed back to the day

When I was locked away

They all tell me

That it was the only way.

Meet your new master, the Queen of Disaster,

She's going to let you know how it goes.

I had to behave, so that I could have a shave

I was lucky to even remember my name.

Every single day, trying to find a way to get out

And I wondered what this was all about.

Every so often, I would hear a shout

Either staff or the committed.

They said I belonged there,

But I refused to admit it.

I still don't know what they dosed me with,

But I took a long, deep sleep.

I woke up so foggy that they knew they could keep me.

Nice and calm now, here's a bunch of questions.

We'll let you know when we think you're alright.

This poem describes nightmares and flashbacks to when I was hospitalized in the psychiatric unit in 2006.

Finally On Top

He was broken down,

Stepped on,

And will be buried in the ground.

But the demons will not go with him.

His soul shined bright as a star

Reflected through a diamond prism.

While alive, he kept marching,

And after every single fall, he got up.

He would not quit and refused to lose.

A battle he didn't get to choose.

A peaceful man, with a warrior's fight

Even though he didn't sleep at night.

The shadows danced wherever he looked,

But he just learned to ignore them.

The voices never stopped either,

But again, he lived through it.

Even he didn't understand why he kept getting up.

Maybe he wanted to be a legend.

Maybe when he's finally at rest,

He wants to be remembered as a man that never gave up.

Maybe he wants to be an inspiration and example

To everyone that is facing hard times.

Although he didn't always understand,

He understood never to stop.

And when it's all said and done,

With any luck,

He will finally end up on top.

This fits the theme about death and being remembered again. I was thinking that when my life is over, I can finally rest and "end up on top". I hope I have left a positive imprint on the world. To me, that's what it means to "end up on top".

Standing My Ground

I will not lay down my sword in defeat.

I will die with it in my hand.

I will not retreat.

You can kill me where I stand.

I've already faced the worst,

So nothing really scares me.

I have nothing to lose,

So all your threats, you can spare me.

I don't back down. I don't quit.

Yes, sometimes I get sick of all of it. I will admit.

But fear and me got to be friends through the years.

So you can speak your negative talk into someone else's ears.

This poem is about staying positive in the face of adversity and not giving up.

You Can't Take Everything

The tears sting sweetly

As they roll down my face.

And things were taken from me

That can't be replaced.

But I'm not bitter or angry or sad.

I can't go on that feeling that way.

But it's still hard to believe

All the words that you say.

Like you love me and you are proud.

Down deep I know them to be true.

But when I hear them out loud,

There's only so much healing they can do.

I wrote this poem after I had been crying. It speaks to how I feel that I am damaged and broken, no matter how much everyone encourages me.

The End

As I watched clouds explode

And stars collide

The sky swallowed itself in submission.

An event for no one's eyes---

But that night

With my mind's permission

I witnessed the grim possibility of the future.

The catastrophic, violent images

Disturbed me enough to retreat

And run from the Creator and Destroyer

No hope for success, the inevitable demise

But that's not what our state implies

And when greed, power, and money combine

They will leave nothing behind.

As soon as I woke

I pleaded to the silence

To never let me see the day

When the sunshine goes away.

This is about a dream I had about the end of the world.

My Resting Mind

Usually when my mind is racing

I write my best

But today my mind is taking a rest.

Not thinking much at all

Unusual for me.

A sense of peace and calm

Bathed in mirth and security.

My thoughts are not frantic

Unusual for me.

Feeling pretty fantastic

But never to the highest degree.

Not too sluggish

Or nerves standing on end.

No negative thinking

And realizing I just bend

Never break.

If I could only find which road to take.

This is describing my usual symptoms and how they are absent while I was writing this. It also alludes to not really having a set direction and general uncertainty with my life.

Paint You a Picture

I tried to paint you a picture.

I'm not much of an artist, but I can get by.

I don't have many secrets left,

Or too many lies.

I told you my feelings that I kept inside.

It seems like so long now.

I wonder who noticed. I wonder who read.

I wonder who chose to ignore it all instead.

I do what I can with what I have.

And I'm giving it all I can.

The words had to come out,

From my head straight out my hands.

I don't ask for much, because I really don't need it

I can do without a lot.

I prefer it that way actually,

Life can make you ill, the more that is sought.

I do better with less. Less mess. Less hassle.

Less stress. Less worry.

But it's still all a little blurry.

I'm feeling my way through

To fight another day.

I wonder if it will all ever go away.

This poem is about how I tried to "paint a picture" of what mental illness looks like in my first book. One last theme that you have seen throughout this book is that I keep fighting and don't give up.

My Lasting Wish

Most of all I wish you joy

Happiness beyond measure

Infinite pleasure

And satisfaction with your life.

Only you are you

And it is who you were meant to be

Don't wish to be someone else

You were made perfectly.

If you should fall, pick yourself up

And I wish for you, an overflowing cup.

Try to be kind and increasingly wise

There isn't much else

As much as I can surmise.

I want for you the very best

And I mean that more than you know

I hope you find a blissful place

A respite, in your mind, you can go.

Don't spend too much time

On sadness and despair

Seconds are precious

And there are no flowers there.

Pick up the pieces, one by one

Until you feel whole

Nothing will ever be perfect

Not everything you can control.

Try to be your best

Every single day

Show the world your greatness

In every single way.

I wanted to end the book with this poem. I truly, from the bottom of my heart, wish everyone the best. Friend or foe. I have no hostility towards anyone. I want every person to be the best that they can be and to try their best. Love and best wishes, always....

Made in the USA
Columbia, SC
22 October 2020